Success Nuggets
for
Your Success

By **Peter Srinivasan**

Table of Contents

Nugget 1: The God, You and the Greatest Gift in the World

God created man in His image. Yes brothers and sisters you heard that right! He created you, me, your dad, mom, your spouse, uncle, friends, your teacher, your mentor, my mentor, and each and everyone in His image.

So what's the point?

Yes there's an important point to drive home! With such an omnipotent and all-powerful God, just imagine how the end product would be? If you asked me who's the only manufacturer that doesn't have a quality control department, I would have said it's the manufacturer who created you and me: **The God.**

His products always exceed any standards under the sun and above the sun! At this very moment, realize that before sending you down to the Earth, he kissed you with all His unparalleled love and said,

> *"My dear child, you are so precious to me that I give you the free-will to choose your destiny and I want you to lead a life that is full of riches that one could ever imagine. From now on, I am going to let you on your own and you are to take control of your life on Earth, live a life that's an epitome of my creation and so, on that day of your last breathe, I would be proud of you, and the next moment you'd be once again living with me, happily. I am giving you a very special and powerful gift that I haven't given to my other creations, which if used properly, would do all the miracles and life-transforming things as if I were with you and could easily overcome any seemingly insurmountable obstacles and challenges. Only thing is, it's up to you my child, because of your free-will, to earnestly realize that you have my gift sitting at the top of your head: Your mind. And that day will mark the dawn of a new era in your life"*

> **- THE GOD**

The only place where it's apt for the "revelation" to come at the beginning is: In your thinking. Today could be that day of revelation for you, and once again to become a courageous and winning child of the all-powerful God. God wants to help you out and this very minute may be that time you have been waiting for!!

One of the greatest thinkers of all time, James Allen, in all his wisdom, said, *"They themselves are makers of themselves."* God created you, but, you create your life, your future and your destiny.

How?

By the quality of thoughts you think about and by the massive action steps you take in the right direction.

This principle is equally applicable to all: Whether you are in your 20's,30's,40's,50's,60's etc. so long you could breathe. That's the only condition from this universe. Today you can start off your journey from that path which God has laid for you and has been waiting for your arrival all these days. His wait is over and so is yours!

From now on monitor your thoughts every now and then. If a negative thought or an unhealthy thought or feeling creeps in to your mind, push it aside as if you were chasing off a wild wolf that bit your beloved ones.

Replace a negative thought with a positive one. Believe that everything could be done and it will be done.

Declare in a high pitch of voice to your problems, predicaments and worries that you have at last discovered your ultimate weapon against them. Enough is enough!

Shout at them that you have become harmonious with the Infinite Intelligence by taking possession of your Aladdin lamp! Challenge and threaten your infliction that you would tear them apart with your divinely sword that is your mind.

Ultimately, prove to this world who you are and of course what you have - The greatest gift in the world: Your Mind!!

Action Steps:

1. We all have invisible protection all the time. You are not alone or an orphan. Remind yourself of this Power.

2. No matter what happens, always stay empowered in thoughts. This means:

   a. Positive thinking

   b. Self-confident thinking

   c. Faith-and-hope thinking

   d. Courage thinking

   e. Plan-formulation thinking

3. Never see yourself as a flaw from God. You are perfect because God created you in His image.

Nugget 2: Find Your Mine and Dig Deeper and Deeper

The Tasmania Gold mine, Australia...

The Battle Mountain Gold mine, USA...

The Beatrix Gold mine, South Africa

The Pokrovskiy Rudnik, Russia...

The Red Lake Gold, Canada...

What do these mines have in common?

They all have "Gold treasures" and obviously they are all hundreds of meters in depth!

Why do people take such a valiant effort to dig deeper?

To find Gold!

What if they don't dig deeper, mostly hundreds of meters?

NO GOLD!

This is the same for every person as well. The same principle applies to life too. Nature has always been conveying some great truth and success principles.

The Gold mines we all have:

The gold mines, the place where you can find your gold. But, to find yours you have to dig deeper. Your gold is your talents, your special interest, your flair, etc.

When you find where your gold mine is (Passion and talent) and start digging deeper and deeper, despite all the obstacles, confusion, discouragement, and adversities that come your way, there's no stopping you!

When you have discovered your gold mine, you move forward on your own initiative without being pushed by anybody or you don't have to live a life following others' dreams. This is where people who have found their goldmines are happiest and fulfilled in the world. They are the ones who are paid a lot money for their expertise.

If you have found your gold mine (your passion area, interests, and special talents) that are also marketable and in demand, you too will become a very happy person and will be paid a lot. But, you must focus all your energy on developing your skills and talents to a world-class level or level of excellence.

Andrew Carnegie, probably the richest man to ever live in the recorded history of the world, whose net worth would be 300+ billion dollars today, once spilled and sprinkled the following pearls for us to ponder,

"You can keep all your eggs in one basket - just watch that basket real closely."

Now what does he mean?

He means that to achieve anything that is really *really* significant and great, one must gather all his or her concentration and resources that have been given naturally to that person and direct them toward a single end or on one single passion or definite major purpose or primary objective in their life.

You have to go deep, like they go deep when finding gold. *Superficial efforts will not produce the desired results.*

When one focuses all his or her energies, thoughts and capital on a single thing, on a single profession that is his or her passion in which he or she has natural ability and interest, that person can expect things that are not normally, under normal conditions expected and accomplished - and monetary rewards are only one of the many rewards one receives by this powerful principle.

Renowned authors like Napoleon Hill and William Walker Atkinson emphasized this truth all through their life, for they knew that men and women have this inherent privilege to live a prosperous and meaningful life!

"God doesn't give you a challenge without giving the equivalent or greater ability to face and overcome the challenge."

It seems that everyone who is born on this planet are assigned a great task or special thing before birth and more importantly, and quite interestingly, also given the attitude and aptitude to carry out their undertaking successfully and to the fulfill their life's purpose, leaving a permanent mark of their stay and accomplishments on this planet.

But somewhere along the line, life threatens them and they completely forget their task on earth, and out of compulsion they start concentrating and supporting on the task that's been assigned to others! Or worse yet, they live a life that is way less than how much they are capable of.

So, the step for you is to find your passion and devote as much time as you can. Nurture it. If you cannot follow it at full swing now, at least start doing something about it. Maybe you have it as your hobby and you can move in that direction gradually. Sometimes, at best, your passion can only be your hobby. That is okay. But devote a set time for it, if possible, everyday.

This can positively affect your main job that you are doing now because as you continue to have time for your passion, your mind starts to get back it's inherent enthusiasm, and that can spill everywhere. And maybe that can pave the way for your passion to be your full-time work in the future. Remember, your passion or talent or your special interest could become your gold mine.

So, what's next after following a certain passion for some time?

Millionaires and billionaires do have diversified streams of income. They are doing service in more than one area and cater to different kind of people and markets. Maybe certain business they have may not be their passion, but they do the business for some kind of fulfillment or for making big profits. However, these same millionaires or billionaires, most of them, would have started their first business based on their passion first, their gold mines.

Nevertheless, before they diversified, they MASTERED HOW TO SERVE ONE TYPE OF PEOPLE FIRST.

In the same way, you too would start concentrating on your passion, developing it, catering one area or a few at first. But, with passage of time, you'd start to diversify yourself finding other avenues of interest with things related to your passion, now rendering service to a wider array of people and in various different areas that are connected to your passion or area of interest.

Find your passion today and start finding things fall in to places.

So, it's time for a Gold Rush!

Nugget 3: Your Belief in Yourself Is in Your Hands

Take a look at history! All that have been achieved were achieved by men and women who thought they could, and by people who believed in themselves *with all their heart*. If you have a child in your home or if you notice the activities of a child, you could understand how it learns many things in such a short time.

Have a child-like self-belief:

A child always concentrates on the things that have to be done and it does them with full conviction that it could do it.

A child doesn't, even for a second, doubt its abilities. It tries … it fails … then tries again … again fails … then tries again … and keeps on trying until it succeeds.

Those successful men and women throughout history, and those today who are very successful, somehow have retained this character from their childhood. They have unshakeable faith in themselves and they take action because of that faith. Even when the physical evidences indicate otherwise. Just like those children they fight like a confident warrior.

Roger Federer has won more than a dozen grand slams. Every time he serves, one could actually see the strength of his mind. He is so convinced that most of the time he can produce an ace and indeed he does produce aces most of the time. And the mind blowing shots he produces seem to come from no where, *but actually it has to do with his belief in himself and in his game.*

Yes, he has natural talent, but even a person who seem to be very "plain" can become a genius with a ton of self-confidence and relentless practice.

These warriors of life always approach life with such an intensity that the fate becomes a loyal pet to them obeying their commands of how they want their life to be lived. Nobody would have served this world like Mother Teresa did. She did things which clearly reflected the power of human potential. She was small in size, but was a monster in self-confidence.

The talents they display were nurtured after they understood what their talents were, followed by harnessing and developing them. But they took massive action in the right direction and grew bigger because of self-confidence in their arsenal.

It is also the other way around, do you know?

When you start to believe in yourself, then this whole world cannot do a thing to stop you in achieving the things that you are destined to achieve. And in the process, you will find your talents and strengths!

Okay, now you may ask me what if I don't have enough self-confidence?

I tell you, "act as if" you are confident for the next few weeks, taking up as many tasks as you can at office and home and do your best to see them through. By the end of these few weeks, you will have the "real" confidence. Action and facing challenges daily will develop an impeccable self-confidence in you. Don't hide from your challenges, ever!

It is because of lack of confidence that you haven't tried much or put a lot of effort. Just do this, just feign confidence and start doing the same tasks that you have thought you could never do.

You will be different or become different if you did so.

What is that inadequate feeling?

There will be some days in a person's life when he or she thinks that they are inadequate. Inadequate for the World, inadequate for their friends and relatives, inadequate for their job or business, inadequate as a husband or wife, etc. This point in their life is the robber which robs their belief in themselves. They start to take a new direction with out knowing it.

If they only knew that it's a temporary mind-set and said that *"This too shall pass"* and *"I am bigger than all my problems combined together."* But they don't do this and instead let the situation control them. As a result, they start to lose their confidence.

The key is to decide upfront that you would not allow these days to touch your confidence.

The phenomenal businessman Henry Ford once said,

"If you think you can do a thing or think you can't do a thing, you're right."

The opposing forces will try to stop you from taking action, from believing in your natural God-given talent (Everybody has one talent at least) and even making you to believe that you were born to be a failure. Even if nothing works on that day, that's okay. Stay confident and believe in your inherent greatness.

Just pick all those negative thoughts up, gather them and go to the nearest trash bin and drop them there. It always will be false and deceiving. When a person couldn't be normally penetrated by all the distractions, then it is a great sign that he or she has mastered the mind and is operating from a high level of thoughts.

No negative, degrading, discouraging information could disturb this super soldier. They all bounce off from his mind like bullets bouncing off from steel. Belief in you is always the starting point to develop that rock hard mind where nothing could penetrate.

Your days will be a history for the future generation and you could very well be an inspirational historical figure for them!

Nugget 4: Sow your seed today and enjoy your own garden tomorrow

Everybody wants to have a rich life that's blessed with everything they need and want. You have been richly blessed with everything you need in order to accomplish your goals you set for yourself. You are not a lamb that leads a mediocre life but a lion that controls a vast territory!

It'll just take you only a few minutes to change the direction of your life, to change yourself from a lamb to a lion. To change one's life doesn't need big shifts but small ones here and there. Just sow little good seeds here and there every day.

Just make a vow to yourself that you will sow as many good seeds as possible. No matter what happens, no matter what the results are, pledge that you will keep on sowing seeds that will benefit you and others.

What do "seeds" mean here? Read further...

You want to become a good dad or mom? Then sow the seed of spending valuable time with your child or children.

You want to be an outstanding student? Then sow the seed of interest, thorough understanding and hard work towards your subjects.

You want to be a better business man? Then sow the seed of persistence, belief, honesty, nurturing people, and constant learning towards your business.

You want to be a good role model to others? Then sow the seed of living your life that even the heavenly beings would get jealous of.

You want to be an expert in whatever you do? Then sow the seed of primarily concentrating your efforts in one single profession and stay there until you succeed or become an expert.

The entrance to your magic garden is already built! Now it's your time to create that garden you want!!

Success Nuggets for Your Success - 12

Whatever you want in your life starts from sowing the seeds towards that goal or goals. This moment could very well be the starting point for all the good things to come. Start taking actions toward your goals. That is your sowing.

You could decide that you are going to sow the seeds by taking consistent daily actions, even if they are small ones, in the direction that would get you happiness, good relationships, money, better health, peace of mind, fulfillment in your life, spiritual satisfaction, mental strength, improved knowledge of anything you want, braveness, humility, etc.

But start taking those small steps towards your goals. Today think of revamping your entire life for better. Little steps lead to big transformation. Sow these little steps starting today.

How much do you want to sow is directly proportional to how much riches that you want to enjoy in your life. However, without sowing there couldn't be a harvest.

From the time you wake up to the time your head hits the pillow, make a vow that you will keep on investing in yourself that you would use each minute every day taking actions for the betterment of your life.

Consequently, your harvest will be a rich one. You'll have more than you could ever handle. Every area will be overwhelmed with blessings that betoken your sincerity and seriousness towards your life.

On your death bed, you'll be well surrounded by a garden that you have created for yourself and you'll be an example for others. All the seeds by then would have grown in to big trees, bearing beautiful flowers and fruits. Your garden would portray the life that you have lived so well.

Even the "Death" would pretend falling asleep on your death bed hesitating to fall up on you.

Sow the good seeds, water them and see for yourself what unfolds!

Nugget 5: Missed your train, hold on, something is coming!

They might have missed their train! They might think it is the last train ever and that they cannot not reach their destination, ever. With closed eyes and tears, they wander inside the train station all through their life without noticing other trains that pass through.

But, the moment they take notice again and start to think that they could reach their destination by the next train, they start to progress towards their destiny.

Unfortunately this world where we live has conditioned us that one could only succeed at an early age or at a certain point of time in life, and if the person has lost an opportunity or missed out a chance, they are doomed for ever!

How false is this notion about life!

This kind of attitude towards life would destruct everything in a man's or woman's life creating a false image of life: An image of darkness and fear instilled in them complemented by a sense of worthlessness. Hopeless feelings take over and kill their confidence and self-worth.

The following quote of power by George Elliot explains how exactly everybody should approach life and what power we have deep inside each of us,

"It is never too late to be who you might have been"

You might have missed an opportunity or opportunities but, *never your potential.* Your divine power, that unique gift from our creator is there, always and it cannot be put out by any adverse conditions or any challenges or defeat in your life. Starting today you can reach any destination and many destinations that you want for yourself.

Don't believe that you are too old to start all over again. Age is a mere number. In the biblical times, there were people who happened to live for many centuries, and more importantly did things that keep on amazing us even today. So be it for you. The societal norms and beliefs are sometimes not only strict but also so misleading and dumb.

Society may tell you that your time is up and you don't stand a chance against your challenges. It may even go on further to inculcate in you that your efforts would be futile if you tried. To prove this is a myth, just seize an opportunity by its collar and utilize it to your best. You'll be surprised that you have always had chance to make it happen.

Don't allow You-have-no-chance disease to take hold of you.

There are some people who waste their opportunity that show up tomorrow by not even trying because they have fixed in their mind that they have missed their train and there is no second chance for them now due to age or lack of experience.

In contrast, there are others who too have missed many opportunities, nevertheless they don't fail to seize an opportunity that comes their way. It is this hope that can take you places.

These people will eventually succeed and would give a come back *because they are trying and bouncing back repeatedly.*

Forget about you past failures and what you have missed out. Make a decision to grab every opportunity that you find. Opportunities used well will change your life.

Just imagine that Thomas Alva Edison had lost his memory at his peak and got it back after several years. What do you think he would do in such a situation?

He'd just start all over again, and still he'd go on to achieve all the things that he had lost, in a short span time of time! He wouldn't care about the lost opportunities rather he would keep his eyes open for current opportunities.

He knew that neither age nor any missed opportunity or any wrong idea about life cannot tie him down. He'd just march forward trampling all these wrong guidelines and notions made up by society.

Not only would he, but every successful man and woman would do the same. They never fret about that missed business opportunity or about "good old days."

They believe that "Better current days" are with them. Everyone always have that good reminiscence of their old times. It's of course, good, but it's a pity sight that these same good people think that their present situation is not in order and as good as the old days. Our days are what we make out of them.

Having good memories of the past, pragmatic action plans for now and a tunnel vision for tomorrow—this single philosophy carries with it the guarantee card for the product of a good life, and the guarantee period is your complete life time.

Maybe you have missed an opportunity but look out, for there's a plane to take you to your destination!

Nugget 6: Voices of labyrinth and your innate strength

They may say that you are good for nothing

They may always try to pull you down

They may scoff at every endeavor you take, great or small

But, it is what you say and think about yourself that counts, every single time...

They may sometimes back stab you

And they will mock at your weaknesses

They have always wanted you to surrender to their will

But it is how you respond to their wicked ways that is more important

They may try to take control of your mind

And without fail they look for ways to sap your vital energy

They will be happy if you have negative self-image

But, it is ultimately where you go for a refuge: to the kingdom of light or darkness

They may poison the faith of your family and friends in you

They may laugh at every slip that you will experience in your life

They will try to sidetrack you from your sincere efforts towards success

But, it is frequently remembering your job on earth that will put you in the driver's seat

Success Nuggets for Your Success - 17

They will hit you suddenly, when least expected, to see your downfall

At times they will shout at you saying that you are a born-failure

They will make sure that you don't take any steps and stay dormant

But it is where you place your confidence that matters— in you or in them

They won't want you to use your treasure that you have in you

They will do in all their power to create a false picture of life

They hurt you and keep on doing it until they could see you are dead

But, beloved, it is knowing that you shouldn't quit, that will terminate them

For these are the negative "inner voices", that little devils that talk to you

Saying and doing all the deeds to hinder you from progressing

From having even a normal life that's your birth right

For these voices of destruction don't know what you have, or what you are!

They chase you until you keep running from them in despair

But... stop abruptly! And turn back, for now they are running away from you

And gone! Gone with the wind!!

For no force of demolition could take you down

When you make an alliance with your real self

Success Nuggets for Your Success - 18

The voices would become voiceless and speechless

And by then all their vices against you are hopeless!

And in your supreme beauty you are spotless!!

Nugget 7: Who is Your Competitor?

Once up on a time, there was a little girl by the name Catherine. She is the only child in her family and the apple of her parents' eyes. One day after school she looked very dejected and her papa asked her what the matter was. She pulled out her report card from her bag and handed it to him. He pondered over her report card and asked her if her sadness had anything to do with her report card. She promptly said yes continuing that she had been outclassed by Sarah, her class mate, who had got A's in all the subjects.

Immediately understanding what her problem was, her papa said to her,

"Dear daughter, I know how hard and sincere you worked. You have got mostly B's in your subjects. You remember where you stood last time. Mostly you had C's right? That means you have improved. Your performance has been better this time. This is to say that you set your own standards *and never worry and compare yourself with others.* I hope you understand what I say my dear"

So it goes with out saying that she went on to become one of the top students in her class, then her college, in her state, and finally in her life.

Most of the pressure and problems are solved *when one stops comparing himself or herself with others,* for each individual is different.

The following 3 principles can set you on the road to a different you.

1. Setting ones own standards is what one needs.

2. Role models can be used as an inspiration but...

3. Your years of pressure are taken off immediately.

1. Setting ones own standards is what one needs:

Whether one works for a company, a student in a school or college, a home maker, a young boy or a girl, a businessman or a businesswoman, or an old person, *life will take a new meaning when they stop to compare their standards with others, their performance with others, their beauty with others, or whatever they have or do or are, with others.* Everyone has different attributes distributed according to their gifts and unique personalities. What one person can do the other person cannot (and don't have to) and vice versa.

It's concentrating on what we can do and not what we cannot do…

It's accepting what we are naturally and what we are not…

It's being who we are and not who we are not…

Every man is handsome in his own ways and in the eyes of God. Every woman is talented and beautiful in her own ways. Human beings have their own gifts and personal world, which they most often fail to discover *because most of the time they are comparing themselves with others. This leaves them no time to discover and develop their own kingdom.*

For instance, say a man compares himself with an athlete and gets bogged down just because he couldn't have the same level of stamina and health. Pitifully, he forgets the fact that it isn't a must to have that much of stamina and health to live, but just a sufficient amount of stamina and healthy body to efficiently carry out activities towards one's goals. Because of this foolish comparison and feeling of inferiority and ignorance, chances are that man wouldn't take action, massive or small, towards acquiring good health and stamina. This is so with all the subjects.

We compare ourselves with others – form wrong beliefs and ideas – then discourage ourselves – start believing we don't have potential – and then, just don't start or we just forget about the dream. All this is because of dumb comparisons.

This comparing and contrasting is the thief that ruins the motivation to take action. Comparison makes life unrealistic.

So what's the key?

When one begins to compare his or her past performance and past self with his present to see how much he or she has changed for the better, that person is on the upward curve in his or her life. Comparing you with yourself is the redemption principle.

When people encounter a person who is doing better, they have to realize that he is a different entity. He or she has nothing to do with your performance or life. That person is striving for his or her excellence, and you, for yours!

Be an island when it comes to comparison. You are your own country or island.

2. Role models can be used as an inspiration but...

Role models or a person whom you want to emulate could be used as an inspiration but not to be compared with ourselves while we are still on the growth curve. If men and women would realize that they don't need to perform at the same high level as their role models during their formative years, then they can save a lot stress. The false comparison would steal all their passion and confidence.

Rather concentrate on your own self, do the necessary work and all of a sudden you may be surprised that you have become your ideal self.

3. Your years of pressure are taken off immediately.

All the pressure that one may experience due to this "comparison mindset" is taken off immediately when one realizes that he or she is different from others and that they don't have to a victim of this comparison syndrome anymore.

You will experience an immediate freedom and weightless feeling when you no more compare yourself with others. This will be obvious when you are at your workplace, with your spouse enjoying a vacation, in a crowd, in a meeting, in a class, in a party, when you socialize with your friends and others, etc.

Surpassing your own old performances should be the goal and not competing with others and comparing with them.

You are your competitor!

Keep raising your standards and forget about others standards!

Nugget 8: People are your mobile libraries

On his or her way towards ones success, an individual becomes more and more knowledgeable, gets more and more bright like a star who is finally finding the niche in this world after having been a serious student of his or her life.

They become increasingly perfect than they were before. Their character, attitude, morality, knowledge, demeanor, etc., become further polished and more matured, and keep on soaring high, that one day it would become a raging fire spreading itself to whoever comes into contact with it.

Overall, they come closer and closer to their ultimate self to which they are capable of. Their life ends on a grand note, that some people around them wonder how they have been able to display such a shining example of a character, and others lament that they couldn't be as great as they are, thinking they are not made of that kind of stuff.

No one is made up of great stuff initially. They BUILD it. They learn from different sources and internalize whatever good they find around.

Many of those people of high competence you see *often have the habit of learning something good from others. Just introduce your dad or friend to these great people and they will not miss the opportunity to learn something good from your dad or friend, even if they were to talk only for a brief time.*

Like a book, which is one of the vehicles to nourish and stuff your brain with all the information you need to revolutionize your current situation, *learning from people is another very effective fantastic way to make yourself more valuable and increase your glow of your character and moral values. As well, it is a great tool to learn some skills from others.*

In spite of their vices, any person is unfailingly and gracefully blessed with something good, that's either very pronounced or ordinary. Get them from them. Get those golden nuggets and make them yours.

There is not even a single person from whom you cannot learn at least one single good character trait or one good idea about life or about your job or business. (In addition, you can also identify the bad things and avoid them in your life)

Make your public place a mobile library that you can read and learn from the walking tomes, which are your inmates of this world—the people around you. Observe them like Sherlock Holmes.

Your home, your office, your school or college, your neighbors, even someone who may despise you can be a pond of water from which you can quench your thirst for knowledge, continually, to become a better you.

One way of efficiently learning something good *is by giving a sincere compliment.* You can make it a habit to identify good points in others and sincerely compliment them. What you compliment others, the same thing you could start internalizing for yourself as well, provided if you like that good thing in that person and would want the trait yours.

The more one sincerely give compliments, the more one can learn and improve.

What one could learn from the people around him or her?

Well, one could learn **discipline, punctuality, stoicism, tolerance, patience, humility, openness, and billions of amazing things from others** (If you learn humility from others, just copy the "virtue" humility and not the way they behave, for you may lose your "own identity" and "being yourself").

One learns a "Virtue" or a character trait and they do it in their "Own" way, and not imitating the gestures and body language of that person from whom that person learns a new virtue or anything useful.

Here's one drop from the ocean of many examples of people who had the habit of learning something from others.

Benjamin Franklin, the brilliant statesman and prolific writer, cultivated 13 virtues, working on one virtue per week. The virtues, by the way, he observed from the men that he thought to be his role models. He tried, till his death, to the best of his ability to abide by these virtues. These virtues contributed enormously to his achievements.

Ask the question, "What are the good nuggets that I can get from this person?" Then, identify the good points, compliment the person honestly, and then note down the virtue and if you like, try to implement it.

Learn from others and become a mobile "good-virtues and great-habits encyclopedia."

Nugget 9: Get a big bite out of this "Cake" and succeed!

There is a big, soft and charming cake that's been handed to all human beings on this planet. Some just nibble the cake throughout their time on this Earth and some would take gentle bites from it.

Still there are very few shrewd ones, who make up only an infinitesimal in number when compared to the other two kinds of people, who gracefully take big bites every time, everyday and even every hour.

Still wondering what this big cake is? **It is your beautiful LIFE** that's longing for your attention to become like a word in a dictionary: Meaningful. More meaningful than it is now!

The bottom line is those few "chosen ones" who manage to take big bite from the cake of life, every single time they go out, *do so by their attitude and extra effort.* They recognize the challenges and obstacles, and despite them they take action. They see the half-glass full.

No doubt, these "Big-biters" would choke unlike the other two who play safe games. But "choking" is a test of your mettle and life rewards these "Go-getters" many times over with her riches from Heaven. These are the people that derive greatest satisfaction and meaning out of this life.

In addition, they are recognized for their valiant acts and some even go a step further to buy a place in the pages of history books, just because they aren't afraid of the "Choke" that is the consequence of the big bites, also called, taking big calculated risks and living life to the fullest and courageously.

Okay, a while ago did I just say "Few chosen ones"?

Yes I did, but what I meant was they were chosen by life because of their "Big bite" approach and attitude and tenacity. They are:

Chosen to be pioneers in every area of life...

Chosen to be blessings to others around them...

Chosen to lead a life that is a paradigm of success...

Chosen to carry out mission that they set for themselves...

And so forth. On the other side of the coin, many men and women who are "Nibblers" and "Moderates" or "Averages" are desperately waiting for the life to reward them without even realizing that they only need to change their approach and attitude(in their "Biting") to make the life come to them and grant them all they need and want. *They got to generously take a big bite from this cake of life.* Life says,

"You take one step towards me and I'll take two towards you"

The good news! Now you can join this group of elite people. Just put on the "Big-biter" robe. Do the things to the best of your ability and never mind in stretching yourself a bit more. Go a mile further than others.

I believe that great men and women are born...as well as made. If you think that you don't belong to the former category, *then go on to create the latter in you.* This is the perfect time! Don't go for the mediocre life which is much in vogue.

This is the day to become a "Chosen one." And without fail, you'll standout from the crowd even while you are humble.

It's not always a bad thing to follow the herd. But the question is, "Which herd are you going to follow"? The "Big-biters" or the "nibblers?"

Now, I can see you are opening your mouth wide to take that "BIG" magical bite!

Nugget 10: Fear, your time is up!

Fear- It strikes a melancholy chord whenever one hears this word. Fear saps the entire energy field in men and women and stops them from achieving big things.

—It poisoned you the moment you embraced it without knowing that it could take your entire life down.

—It poisoned you when you were told by someone that you were not as good as others. You believed their casually-tossed remarks very seriously and took them to your heart. That's your day of inauguration with your FEAR.

—It poisoned you when you were at your school as a kid, and was told by someone that you are different from others and inferior to them.

—Again this thief poisoned you when you participated in that college event. You were falsely whispered in to your ears by him that you were not worth the prize, and worse yet, not even the participation.

—He got in your way once again when you got a job, injecting in you the poison that you cannot do the job well, cannot handle even the petty issues, and worst of all is that your boss was a demon and you were his or her slave. So you were ill-at-ease each and every day at your office, just getting by, just crawling.

—It interfered in your marriage life, in your spiritual life, when you were in front of an audience, each time you come face to face with your wealthier neighbor. You cringed in front of others.

To add fuel to the fire, it is present in each and every activity of your life, intervening between you and success. Simply put, it is working round the clock to destroy you completely.

Why is this so? Why such a gloomy life?

Because "Fear" has made it a point to accompany you ever since you ignorantly gave an invitation to him. He accompanies you wherever you go.

This thing has played and has been playing the "Spoil game" in every area of your life and *has confined you to a small dungeon of inferiority complex and false beliefs. It has created a false image that your are useless, worthless and spinless.*

It literally cornered you! It has been chasing you everywhere you go!! Whatever undertaking, whatever endeavor, whatever venture you take to make your life a flourishing one, this Satan comes to the spot and seizes you by your shirt collar and imprisons you.

It sleeps with you and it is even by your side when you take a shower. It visits your mind whenever you attend a party, big or small, and rips you off, making people to laugh at you!

He sits in your head when you visit a dental clinic. He is with you, creating doubts in you, when you think of going to a gym to get into shape. He is with you when you are thinking of changing your career.

When you are in your examination hall he is with you creating "Hopelessness" in you.

The "fear" surrounds you even when you are in a public place, shopping, making you an introvert. He is more severe in old-aged men and women.

You think that you cannot do a thing about it, whereas in reality, you are the master and he will run away from you the moment you realize this. The moment you realize that he has nothing to do with you.

The moment you realize that he has already done severe damages to your life and you are no more going to allow him to do those same filthy acts by making you a coward.

Think of all the times you missed out opportunities, failed to ask somebody for something which could have changed your life, held back from trying something out, and many more things in your life—just because you FEARED!

Once, a long time ago, the FEAR captured you. *But by then you were only a child, or at least ignorant.* But no more are you ignorant. You know you can and, you will! Now you know what you are capable of doing back to your fears!!

For you are no ordinary living being that surrenders his or her life in to the hands of fear and fate. You are a human being—the ultimate creation of God. Yes the ultimate creation of God!! You shouldn't submit to this small thief.

Your old ways and old thinking patterns, which has held you in captivity for all these years, should be burned down now!

Within you is a family that consist of opportunities, positive thinking, good health, wealth, well-being, rugged mental health, and peace of mind. And don't allow this culprit "FEAR" to kill off your family.

The great self-help guru Orison Swett Marden said in a tone that is full of longing to relieve you and me from this negative factor called FEAR. He said, *"Fear demoralizes character, destroys ambitions, induces or causes disease, paralyses happiness in self and others, and prevents achievement. It has not one redeeming quality"*

How true are those words! As true as the sun and the star's existence!!

Gather all your resentment against this black force called "Fear" and once for all, tell yourself that "I have had enough from this monster. I know God hasn't intended me to be a coward and fear all those silly things. I am natural if I don't live in fear each and everyday. I am very powerful and hereby I declare that I have overcome my "Fears" and they are now under my feet, lying dead."

More riches, more happiness and no more FEAR!

Nugget 11: Hand death certificate to your timidity and shyness

You are in this world to be courageous and to do valiant acts. Every soul should lead a life that is full of serenity and not timidity. **Your wait is over.**

Declare to yourself that you are a man or woman who's born to lead your life like every other person in the society and not to have many deaths each day from the time you wake up from your sleep.

Now, think about these questions:

Why do you think you are inferior to others?

Why do you assume that you are making mistakes while others not?

Why do you think that you are inadequate?

What makes you believe that God created you a weakling?

Which evil force is creating a false illusion in you that you are worthless and that everyone is after you?

And how come your friends seem to enjoy the get-together and you are not?

Why are you holding yourself back at every opportunity at your office or working place, whereas deep down in you, you know that you are missing out an important ingredient in your life?

Why are you afraid to move freely with your teachers and classmates in your school?

Now you can change the scenario if you think that you must change it. Remember the world is too busy in doing its work. People are too busy doing their jobs. All of us have but only one life to live. Then why allow your timidity and shyness to stop from doing your daily activities excellently and freely?

The question is:

"Why, my dear, you live your only life in timidity. Why be a shy, fearful boy or girl, man or woman?"

Isn't this the time to get rid of timidity?

The following 3 pillars of truth about timidity will make the change in you.

1. By your timidity you are *focusing on the unwanted*.

2. Realize that you have *your unique you* inside you.

3. Making mistakes are okay. *Everybody does*.

Let's analyze:

1. By your timidity you are focusing on the unwanted:

Men and women, you are actually sabotaging your progress by the direction of your thoughts and focus. You know what, all the successful people concentrate on the job at hand and other trivial things cannot get their attention. Never!

But, remember this...just remember this. Timid people most of the times think what others are thinking about them and are always filled with "fear" and "self-conscious" thoughts. They are the exact opposite of how the highly successful people behave, think and act.

In the long run, these shy people don't learn much because they concentrate on the trivial things *rather than on the main ones,* maybe during their school days, or during their years in the college, or worse, unfortunately, even after they become an adult and are now in workforce.

They have lost their natural behavior they once had and every time they go out, they are not not being natural. This is a big mistake. Being natural and free is your birth right. When you are shy and timid, you are having some big resistances inside you that can slow you down a lot. You go as fast as you can only when you find your natural self.

From this moment onwards focus your attention on the job, and never mind about what others think about you and all those trivial matters.

When a timid person starts concentrating on the job at hand, on the issue, rather than on the people, they can make an immediate shift in their life.

2. Realize that you have your unique "you" inside you.

There is only one you in the whole universe, even if you are one of the twins, triplets or even quadruplets.

Many tender-hearted people are made to change their natural inborn qualities for others– I mean, the way they naturally speak, act and even feel. They are compelled. They are forced and pushed since their childhood up until their death.

But don't succumb to the external forces! Don't!! Don't let this world to manipulate you to change you according to their wish. Be yourself! This world always tries to make you a puppet. Don't allow them to put strings on you.

Just because you are silent, introvert in nature doesn't mean that you are to be timid. Many successful men and women who are musicians, scientists, doctors and even actors are introvert but are not timid. There is a difference.

Introvert may go to a party, be calm and might still enjoy the party. But if one is timid and introvert, he or she will be in distress all the time at the party.

So, you may be naturally an introvert person. Just be like that. Don't try to wear the mask of the "Extrovert" and act like an extrovert, imitate them and in the process lose your "REAL SELF".

Rather just keep improving yourself and keep strengthening your social skills so that you can be very effective, even if you are an introvert naturally. Don't try to blindly act like others.

You can be an introvert and still have friends, wealth, happiness etc. Just like all the five fingers are different so are the people on this planet.

Some are introvert, some are extreme introverts, some are extroverts, some are extreme extroverts and most of them are ambivert. It's a false notion that you could be successful only if you are an extrovert. It's a myth. Nevertheless, don't be timid!

Remember all your talents can come to the front only when you are yourself. Just recall the times when you were at your peak: All those times you were very comfortable and were yourself. Isn't it? That's how it works for all the human beings.

Many become timid because they think they should be the person that others would like them to be. Or they think that they must act like that gregarious Joe, if they want to get others' approval.

But, in reality others would automatically like you if you start to be yourself. Always be like that:

Act the way you act naturally

Think the way you think naturally

And be yourself!

And one fine point here: If your natural self is lacking something, just improve on it. That's all. Don't change yourself and act like someone else. For instance, like said before, if you think that you need to become a socially more polished person, just learn those skills and apply them daily. But, never sacrifice your natural self.

3. Making mistakes are okay. Everybody does

Timid men and women suffer a lot just because they think that they are the only ones making mistakes and that others are perfect without a flaw.

The rule is: Mistakes and corrections are the way of life, whether the mistake is a small one or a big one. It's a sad fact that some may go even a step further and become so self-conscious. They notice in themselves even the minute details such as:

Whether the way they hold a pen is right or not...

Whether the way they walk is perfect or not...

Whether the way they talk is impressive or foolish...

As a result, these shy and timid folks become even more timid and shy and this continues until they do something to break it.

Just remember all the person you know and have ever known have made mistakes...a lot of them, and are continuing to make mistakes in their daily life... It's nature.

One learns by mistakes. So the mistakes are the stepping- stones to your success. The more mistakes you make and correct, the more successful you'll become in that endeavor.

Fix these principles in your mind strongly, and you will start to be a different person in a blink of an eye!

Start the second part of your life- The courage one!

Nugget 12: Substitute hard work for ——-?

Sometimes we need to substitute or replace one thing for another in order to get better results and at other times we may want to substitute things to make life easier.

If you want you could replace an old car with a new, more comfortable one. If you don't like your smart phone you could get another model. Likewise, if you are angry you can replace it with love or patience or both.

This great virtue hard-work which can lift anyone on the face of this planet to enormous heights in their life, regardless of their background and education, cannot be replaced or substituted with anything.

There is no substitute for hard work. Many people who started out their life as under dogs emerged as super dogs (Elite man or woman) with just a few elements they essentially had in their arsenal and one of the most powerful among them is: HARD WORK.

They really accomplished what they really thought wasn't possible when they started out their life. But with hard work as their major tool and hope, they overcame many odds and proved to the world that they deserved what they achieved.

Hard work may seem like it is a strain and laborious thing but the fact is, with the passage of time and relentless hard work, one would start to keep on rolling in any endeavor as if he or she has discovered a magic wand.

They would discover many of their hidden talents in the process of industriously working towards a particular goal or goals, which otherwise would be latent all through their life. *Hard work brings talent to the surface and polishes it like a diamond.*

More often than not, it is this piece of the puzzle that eludes many people who are very eager to touch the zenith. It could also be said that hard work is essentially present in all the pieces of the puzzle. It is the essence. Without hard work, other pieces of the success puzzle will lack that "push", that "Master touch."

"Sweat, sweat, sweat and that's your life's best bet

You are now wet, wet, wet and everything for your success is set, set, set!

And there you go, piercing the sky like a jet, jet, jet!"

The satisfaction that one drives from working hard is boundless and inexplicable *unless it is experienced by the individual personally*. Life will be fulfilled.

The Bible says,

Do you know a hard working man? He shall be successful and stand before kings!

Proverbs 22:29

(Applies for both men and women)

Hard work in the right direction with a lot of innovative thinking will make you smart. He or she will proceed or advance quickly and strongly. Hard work actually often transforms one into a smarter human being and mentors him or her to take smart steps. Hard work teaches one gradually how to do a thing in the best fashion and in an optimal way.

The products that come from hard work will withstand the test of time. Michelangelo's work is paragon of what effect hard work could produce to the person who utilizes it, as well to others who's been fascinated towards it. So are the works of Beethoven and Steve Jobs. Even time wouldn't be able to use it's eraser against a work that's a result of hard work, diligence and excellence.

If luck was a big concert then hard work's a VIP who is most welcome. Wherever there's hard work, luck seems to beg for a companionship with it.

"Perspire today; inspire others tomorrow and you won't expire forever."

- Children's Classics
- Self-Help/Philosophy/Motivational Classics
- Timeless Classic Novels and Novellas

— — — — — — — — — — — — — — — — — — —

Timeless Classics for Your Collection

Classic Books for Your Inspiration and Entertainment

——————

Visit Us at:

goo.gl/U8oLCr

— — — — — — — — — — — — — — — — — — — —

Books by:

Jane Austen

Brontë Sisters

Elizabeth Gaskell

Arthur Conan Doyle

Jack London

Louisa May Alcott

Edith Nesbit

L Frank Baum

Mark Twain

James Allen

Stephen Crane

Charles F. Haanel

Lewis Carroll

Jules Verne

Charles Dickens

and Others!

www.ingramcontent.com/pod-product-compliance
Lightning Source LLC
Chambersburg PA
CBHW071310280526
45788CB00004B/1873